Lucy Taylor

The Story of Hedley Vicars

The christian Soldier

Lucy Taylor

The Story of Hedley Vicars
The christian Soldier

ISBN/EAN: 9783337132651

Printed in Europe, USA, Canada, Australia, Japan

Cover: Foto ©ninafisch / pixelio.de

More available books at **www.hansebooks.com**

HEDLEY VICARS

The Story of

HEDLEY VICARS

The Christian Soldier

BY

LUCY TAYLOR

Author of " The Children's Champion, and the Victories he Won,"
" Going on Pilgrimage," " Fritz of Prussia,"
&c. &c.

" Endure hardness as a good soldier of Jesus Christ."
2 Tim. ii. 3.

T. NELSON AND SONS

London, Edinburgh, and New York

1896

CONTENTS.

CAPTAIN HEDLEY VICARS,

CHAPTER I.

FOR QUEEN AND COUNTRY.

WHAT boy was ever known to welcome *Black Monday?* To count up the number of days to the holidays and joyfully watch them slip by, one by one, may be good fun enough; but to find the holidays are over, and to get ready for a return to school, is quite another matter. However pleasant school-life may be when one fairly gets into the swing of it, nobody likes saying good-bye to the dear home, and the last kiss to mother is apt to give a fellow a horrid lump in the throat, and to bring on a watery condition of the eyes, productive of much blinking; though we wouldn't, for the world, have any one guess that there was the slightest suspicion of *tears* anywhere about. How gladly, too, one hails any unexpected hindrance that is good enough to crop up, and how unwillingly one undertakes any share in the dismal preparations for departure.

"Hedley, my boy, you can pack your play-box; the rest of your things will soon be ready," said Mrs.

One day, for instance, we find him retreating to a little cave in the garden, barricading the entrance so that no one could follow him, and announcing that there he intended to spend the night! And all because he had behaved ill at family prayer, and his mother had reproved him. However, there *is* an end to this story, and a very satisfactory one; for we are told that the young hermit's offended dignity gave way at last before the entreaties of his little sisters, and, somewhat ashamed of his ridiculous conduct, he crept back to the house, humbling himself to ask pardon for his foolish trick, and finding his own little bed much more comfortable quarters than the dark, damp, draughty cave, romantic as it looked in the sunlight.

Hedley's home was in Ireland. He was not an Irish boy, however; for he was born, on the 7th of December 1826, in an island on the other side of the Equator, the Mauritius, off the east coast of Madagascar. But the boy came home with his mother and sisters while quite young, although his father was detained abroad by his duties as a soldier till Hedley was nine years old, when he returned to Ireland, and died four years afterwards. Our hero's full name was Hedley Shafto Johnstone Vicars. The family from which he was descended was a Spanish one, Don Vicaro having come over from his sunny land of oranges nearly four hundred years ago, when Katherine of Aragon sailed north as the bride of our Prince Arthur; this princess afterwards became the ill-fated wife of our fickle king, Henry VIII.

When Hedley lost his father, his love for his widowed mother seemed to grow stronger and

tenderer than ever, though it could not exactly be
said that he always gave the best proof of affection
by loving to do those things she would approve.
Mr. Vicars, when dying, had laid his hand upon the
lad's head, and prayed that he might be "a good
soldier of Jesus Christ." But Hedley gave little heed
to the fulfilment of the prayer; he was much more
eager to "enjoy life," as he called it, and to do as he
liked, than to ask himself what his work in the
world was to be, and why he had been sent here at
all. At school he paid scant attention to his lessons,
and indeed was so full of pranks that he even
persuaded one of the younger masters to join him in
adventures which did neither of them any credit
Time was thus thrown away which was, long after,
bitterly regretted; for while at Woolwich, studying
for a soldier's career, idle habits, once indulged in,
had become so strong that the young student failed
in passing examinations which would have fitted him
for a higher branch of army service than he afterwards entered.

Not that the young soldier had any distaste for
his profession. He loved it and was proud of it;
only, like so many others, he foolishly shirked much
of the drudgery that would have laid the foundation
for honours and advancement. When seventeen years
of age, he attended his first review, having by that
time entered the army, and joined the 97th Regiment
in the Isle of Wight. Marching and manœuvring
and firing he found very fatiguing exercises; but the
excitement and the gaiety of the scene were inspiring,
and in a letter to his mother he says, "My zeal for the
service kept me up." The young soldier was proud

of his trim uniform; and when he returned home, a
few months later, to Essex, where the family were
then living, he won the warm admiration of his
sisters, his bright face and handsome, upright figure
setting off to great advantage the smart military
dress. The visit was one of farewell, and doubtless
tried the mother's heart sorely, though her son might
be too much engrossed with the pleasant prospect
before him of travel and adventure to dwell very
much on the painful necessity of leave-taking.

The 97th was ordered to Corfu, an island off the
west coast of Turkey. The voyage out was a delightful one, much more pleasant than sailing across
the broad Atlantic, when for weeks there would have
been nothing in sight but a wide expanse of heaving
water. The weather was fine, and after passing
through the boisterous Bay of Biscay, which happened
to be in a calmer mood than usual, the grand
Rock of Gibraltar came in sight, and ushered the
voyagers into the beautiful Mediterranean, crowded
with the craft of many nations. Every day was full
of delight to Hedley, for there was always something
fresh to be seen; and then, unlike many young fellows
of his age, he found almost as much pleasure in
beautiful scenery as in exciting adventure. Besides,
he never cared to be idle, and was always ready to
give the sailors a helping hand, though, no doubt,
occasionally making some foolish blunders, and be-
traying his ignorance of seafaring ways.

Corfu is one of the most lovely of all the Ionian
Isles, although its trees, to be sure, are of a soberer
tint than those of old Ireland. It is quite small,
only forty miles long, and at its widest end, the

north, only twenty miles broad. Mulberry trees
grow freely, but the greater part of the island is
covered with dark olives, broken here and there by
still more sombre clumps of cypress. Though it
lies so close to Turkey, Corfu belongs to Greece, and
some traces of the old Greek paganism remain in
a ruined temple. But although its altar-fires have
long since died out, and its pillars are crumbling to
decay, idolatry, alas, still possesses the island, the poor
ignorant peasantry bowing down to pictures in the
numerous Greek churches, and receiving from their
priests the stones and husks of a vain superstition,
instead of the bread of life contained in the Word
of God.

But the darkness of the deluded worshippers
around him did not at all disturb the mind of the
young English soldier; for, in spite of all the teach-
ing received in a Christian home, and the bright
example of those who loved Christ and rejoiced in his
service, Hedley thought of very little beyond his own
personal amusement whenever set free from military
duties. The little Bible his mother had given him
was not only unread but totally forgotten, and very
soon lost in hurried movements from place to place :
letters home were few and brief ; and conscience
sometimes whispered that the scenes of gaiety he
loved were not exactly those into which he would
care to bring his mother and sisters. " I would give
worlds," he writes in later years, " to undo what I
then did."

CHAPTER II.

FOR SELF AND SIN.

HEDLEY VICARS did not spend all his time at Corfu during his stay in the Mediterranean, military duties taking him both to Cephalonia and Zante, though he had no opportunity of seeing the *west* coast of Greece until some years later.

His first stay at Zante was but a short one, lasting only three days, but he writes of it as a "delightful trip;" for he would never suffer to pass unnoticed any of the beauties of the pretty little island, with its broad fertile plain covered with olives, figs, myrtles, orange-trees, pomegranates, and an abundance of lovely flowers, its trim corn-fields and acres of vineyards, from which we are supplied with tons of the useful "currants" so popular in England. When Hedley Vicars visited the island with his regiment it was under British protection, but has since been handed over to Greece, to whom indeed it seems that it should rightfully belong. Perched above the town of Zante, on the east coast, stands the castle; and it was here that some men of the 97th were quartered when Vicars paid the first brief visit that delighted him so much.

On the way back to Corfu he writes to his mother from the island of Cephalonia describing his pleasure. While there he would be in the midst of rocky hills and dark pine woods, with the great Black Mountain rising 5,000 feet, and wearing its cap of snow long after spring was scattering flowers in the valley beneath.

Not long after, Hedley Vicars was quartered again in the Castle of Zante, to his immense satisfaction ; for he found the island "a perfect garden of roses," and was charmed with all his delightful surroundings. Pleasant, however, as everything seemed at the time, the young soldier afterwards looked back upon those days of pleasure as "a hideous blank," just because, amid scenes of earthly beauty, he had missed and put away from him the best treasure, the Rose of Sharon and the Pearl of great price, and so had lost during those early years the joy that might have made his young life blessed, and happy, and useful. Debts, too, were incurred at this time which afterwards caused not a little bitter remorse ; for Hedley Vicars made the acquaintance of some very friendly, hospitable people, and in joining them in amusement and visiting he spent a good deal more money than he could afford, and was dreadfully ashamed to have to own these debts to his widowed mother.

But a soldier's life is ever a restless, roving one, and about three years after its arrival in the Mediterranean the 97th Regiment was ordered right away to the other side of the Atlantic Ocean. But a stay was first made at Malta, that island so familiar to every English regiment that sails eastward, for it contains the largest garrison of any British colony, and is a very strong military station.

The voyage across the Atlantic was not nearly so interesting as the one to Corfu, for after passing Gibraltar scarcely anything was to be seen till the vessel reached the West Indies. Vicars tells us that, until they entered the Caribbean Sea at the end of the voyage, they saw only two vessels, while in the

Mediterranean they had passed hundreds. A big
whale, or a " school " of rolling porpoises, were quite
welcome visitors, breaking the wide stretch of waters
with their strange and awkward antics, and attracting
every one's attention. As before, Vicars was always
ready to coil a rope or climb a mast, and, indeed,
wore sailor's dress that he might the better perform
sailor's duties. He had to take his turn, too, in keeping watch, and many a solitary midnight hour was
passed aloft among rattling cordage and groaning
timbers, with the wind howling all around, and
snatches of fitful moonlight flitting across the dark
waters below. Thoughts of home thronged the mind
of the young soldier in these lonely hours, and
thoughts too, sometimes, of the wasted past, and the
folly and thoughtlessness of the last two or three
years. Very good resolutions, doubtless, were also
formed ; but when back among gay companions. a
mocking laugh or an idle jest served to brush them
all away, unheeded and forgotten.

The 97th on reaching Jamaica landed at Montego
Bay, on the north-west. It is possible to land on
this fruitful island almost anywhere, for there are no
less than sixteen harbours. Plenty of bridges, too,
must be needed inland, for there are a hundred and
fourteen rivers and streams flowing down from the
steep hills. Hedley Vicars' first duty was to conduct a night march, his company being sent to Fal-
mouth, another harbour about twenty miles off. The
march was not without its dangers, for the night
was not only very hot but intensely dark, and although numbers of negroes went with the soldiers,
carrying torches, the men were in constant peril of

falling over precipices close to the road, and as the path wound higher it became exceedingly rough and steep, making it by no means easy to go forward in safety. One man, indeed, *did* fall over at a most dangerous spot, but fortunately caught in some bushes, and was thus saved from being killed, though the march was delayed for half-an-hour while his companions sought him out, and hauled him back on to the road again.

Of course it was not possible to see much of the country, though the travellers could just make out that it was abundantly wooded. The island, indeed, abounds in timber-trees of almost every kind, besides numbers of tropical plants and fruits, and no doubt the path followed by the soldiers was bordered, could they but have seen them, with the loveliest palms and ferns. But if little could be seen much could be heard, insects keeping up an incessant chirping and buzzing. One kind, the fire-flies, even made themselves visible by their curious flickering light. There are no less than fourteen kinds of this one insect in Jamaica, so we are hardly surprised when Vicars tells us that they flitted across the path " by myriads."

One halt was made on this night-march for refreshment, after which there was some severe uphill work ; and no doubt the weary men were glad enough to join their comrades of the 38th at last at Maroon Town, a military station nestling amid lovely trees, and perched in a little dell 2,500 feet above the sea. Here Vicars must have found quite as delightful quarters as in beautiful Zante ; for he tells his mother of his pretty little cottage with its garden and arbour, and of building a house for his poultry, and doing quite a brisk trade in fresh eggs. The luxury, too, of a bath twice a day in a big tank is greatly enjoyed. On the death of a brother officer Vicars removed into his cottage, embowered in honeysuckle and jasmine, which creepers, however, he cut back, as they darkened the windows; but he rejoices in the garden and the bamboo summer-house, and longs to transport his house and himself to his dear home in Essex. Fond of pleasure he still was, but certainly not lazy, for he never missed the mountain breeze at half-past five in the morning ; and there were signs, too, that the voice of conscience was not entirely unheeded, when it whispered silent reproofs for wrong-doing. He has a vague idea, too, that he is not " prepared " for death should it come to him suddenly, far from home and friends, as it did to his young companion ; and he hopes that, " with God's help," he has " learnt a lesson from this sudden death."

But young Vicars had not yet tasted the joy of forgiveness and of Christ's service. He was not, it is true, entirely heedless any longer, but, because he would not surrender to God altogether, he had just enough religion to make him miserable. He attended public worship regularly, and had the opportunity of hearing the preaching of a faithful servant of God ; and, what was perhaps much more important, he saw a good deal of a family who did not merely make a loud profession, but daily *lived* as Christian people should, showing the world a little of the real thing, not holding their Master up to scorn by acting a miserable, transparent sham.

Locks of his mother's and his sister's hair are welcomed by the son and brother as priceless possessions, his joy over these little treasures showing how very deeply in his heart dwelt the love of home and dear ones: few boys go far wrong in the end who can thus remember "home" and "mother." Actions, too, spoke louder than words about Vicars' love for his mother; for he was now saving every possible penny to pay off his few remaining debts, and was exultant at the idea of very soon getting clear of the wretched burden he had been foolish enough to hang round his own neck.

But there was another burden not so easily laid down. The burden of sin weighed heavily: the pilgrim was looking with longing eyes toward the wicket-gate, and even raising his hand tremblingly to knock; but the Cross and its shining ones were not yet in sight. The young soldier, however, was beginning now to feel his own weakness in the face of temptation, and was seeking the aid of the Holy Spirit, so we may be sure "Help" was at hand watching for him. Many quiet hours were spent in thought and reading in his pretty summer-house, as once they had been on the wide ocean, only now all was fragrant and beautiful instead of wild and dreary. Sweet heliotrope and geranium bloomed abundantly in the delicious climate, and tiny sparkling humming-birds flashed in and out among the tall, jointed bamboos. "Even the purring of my little kittens," he writes, "is pleasant to me at such a time;" but adds, after telling of his desire for something better, "I wish I *felt* more what I write."

But these efforts at doing better, made as they were apart altogether from the grace of the Saviour, ended again and again in failure. For a while Vicars was ordered to another part of the island, where he was mixed up a great deal with careless and profane companions, and nothing but the grace of God, which he had not yet accepted, could have kept him from yielding to sin under such strong temptation. Prayer and the Bible, therefore, were again neglected, and it seemed as if the young pilgrim had turned his back altogether upon the narrow way of life. But it was not so. Conscience, silenced for a while, spoke again with yet keener reproaches, and the Scriptures were carefully studied, not only alone, but in company with a Christian friend in the same regiment.

Soon after this the pretty home was left behind, and Hedley Vicars set forth once more on the ocean, this time, however, not for so long a voyage. The 97th had been ordered to Nova Scotia, and in the summer of 1851 landed at Halifax.

CHAPTER III.

ALTOGETHER FOR CHRIST.

THERE was no settling down into barracks for Hedley Vicars on first arriving in Halifax; he was sent off at once to Canada to command some volunteers. In his journal he tells us with what delight he enjoyed an expedition to the magnificent falls of Niagara; for although he had seen much in his travels that was very beautiful, there had been nothing so grand and awful as this mighty rush of roaring, seething waters, either in the lovely Mediterranean isles or in those of the West Indies. He wonders, as he returns day after day to watch the great river taking its mighty leap, and tossing up its cloud of snowy spray, how any one could possibly declare, in the face of such a scene, that "there is no God." Silent and awestruck, he resolves once more not to waste the life God has given in a selfish search after pleasure. But it is not by the thunder of the cataract that God would speak to the heart of the young soldier, and call him to his service. Like Elijah on Horeb, Vicars stands among the wild grandeur of nature and listens to its mighty voices. But the Lord is not in the earthquake, nor in the wind, nor in the fire, nor in the flood. The "still, small voice" has yet to speak.

And the gentle call was not long delayed. His duty in Canada finished, Hedley Vicars returns to his regiment at Halifax, and one evening is found waiting in barracks for a brother officer. A Bible lies at hand, and he listlessly opens its pages, not in anxious search, as he had often done before, but more to while away the few minutes he may be kept waiting. The pages are turned, till the first chapter of John's first epistle lies open, and those well-known words catch the eye of the reader, suddenly fixing his attention (possibly they were marked, and thus more conspicuous)—"The blood of Jesus Christ his Son cleanseth us from all sin."

Vicars read no more. He shut the book; not because his friend had arrived, nor because he was weary of a well-worn subject, but because the words had suddenly struck him as so great and so wonderful that they were as much as he could think of for the time. "If this is true," thought he, "if Christ's atonement really can and does take away all my sin, I cannot ever have anything to do with it again, to

live in it, or delight in it. I must live as one washed
in the blood of the Lord Jesus."

Possibly when his friend joined him Vicars found
little to say—he was so taken up with these wonderful
words, spoken by the still, small voice of the Spirit of
God, that he could think of nothing else; and that
night he slept but little, wondering much whether he
might really say that *his* sin was forgiven, and henceforth have peace within, in spite of all the storms and
troubles that might cross his path. With the morning dawn there sprang up the warm, bright rays of
the Sun of Righteousness. Hedley Vicars felt that
indeed the guilt of the past was, for Christ's sake,
blotted out for ever. "What I have to do," said he,
"is to go forward. I cannot return to the sins from
which my Saviour has cleansed me with his own
blood."

And now began the conflict. "In *me* ye shall
have peace," said Jesus, "but in the world ye shall
have tribulation." Satan never willingly lets one of
his captives slip. "Thou art one of my subjects,"
said Apollyon to Christian; "I am an enemy to the
Prince, and I am come out on purpose to withstand
thee." To profess the name and the service of Christ
among gay officers and blaspheming men was indeed
no easy task, and Vicars well knew that he would
meet a fierce fire of ridicule, if he meant to stand his
ground. But, happily, he did not make the fatal
mistake of hiding his colours, or of trying, for the
sake of peace, to be a secret disciple of his Lord, and,
while enlisting under the banner of the Cross, to
pretend still to be serving the devil. On the very
morning when he gave himself wholly to Christ as

his captain, Vicars boldly bought a Bible; not a tiny pocket volume that could easily be poked out of sight, but a good-sized book that nobody could miss seeing. This he placed open on his sitting-room table. "It was to speak for me," said he, "before I was strong enough to speak for myself."

And very soon it spoke loudly enough, for this old-fashioned book was not at all in favour in the barracks. Former companions dropped off with a sneer or a shrug, or passed Vicars by without a word of recognition. One remarked contemptuously that he had "turned Methodist;" another jeered him openly at "mess," before the rest of the officers; while a third actually accused him of hypocrisy, and of setting up for a "saint," declaring it was the worst of all the bad things he had ever done! Of course nobody could believe such a charge for long. There is no such thing as sham Christianity in camp, for as there is nothing to be gained by an empty profession, there is no temptation to act the hypocrite. Nothing but the *real* thing can live a day among soldiers.

But Vicars was not left to fight his battle entirely alone; God's servants never are. A few other Christian officers gladly welcomed him; and there was the good Dr. Twining, too, the chaplain of the garrison, with whom he soon formed a close and warm friendship. Dr. Twining saw a good deal of his young friend, for Vicars not only attended all the services and Bible-classes, but in the early part of 1852 came to his house frequently. A lieutenant had been very badly hurt while out moose-hunting, and was laid up at Dr. Twining's. Hedley Vicars, anxious now to help and comfort others more than to please

himself, often went to sit with the invalid, and talked
to him, of course, of his own new-found joy. If the
young Christian had found Christ's service a dull and
gloomy thing, cutting him off from all pleasure, and
clouding his life, a question asked by the sick man
one day would have proved a very awkward one.
"Vicars," said he, "tell me, do you *really* feel happier
now than you did?" Not only could Vicars gladly
answer, "Yes, indeed" with his lips, but his sunny
face, his cheerful manner, and his unfailing good-
humour, told every one he met what a happy thing
it was to give one's life to God.

The lieutenant grew worse, and his leg had to be
taken off, Vicars still nursing him with the greatest
care and tenderness, until he at last recovered ; a
cripple, to be sure, for life, but henceforth, like his
kind friend, a disciple of the Lord Jesus. Vicars not
only visited the sick, but taught in the Sunday school,
and took great interest in the work of the Bible and
Missionary Societies, besides reading and praying with
the men of his own regiment, several of whom were
brought to the Saviour's feet through his persuasive
words. And many of those who did not choose to
follow the Christian example of their officer, admired
him for his outspoken conduct, and respected his
wishes and example sufficiently to abstain from
swearing, at all events in his hearing.

By this time Vicars was promoted in the army,
being made adjutant of his regiment, a post, however,
which he afterwards resigned. His colonel told him,
when offering the appointment, that he was the man
he could best trust with responsibility. So, after all,
"pure religion" counted for *something*, even from a

worldly point of view, as, indeed, it always does in the end. It is true one of the officers said, "He won't do for it—he's too conscientious;" but nobody ever found that a careful regard for his duty to his God ever interfered with his duty to his Queen and country.

As we might suppose, Vicars now writes home much more frequently and freely. In April 1852, he tells his sister Mary how hard he has been fighting against sin, and wishes he could show the same spirit in Christ's service that he once manifested in the cause of the devil. "Would that I felt as little fear," he says, "of being called a Christian, as I used to feel in being enlisted against Christianity." He speaks, too, of communion with God, but bemoans that the joy of it is so soon driven away. "My summer-heart of warmth and love changes back into its natural state of winter, cold and dead." But he rejoices to tell of the conversion of one of his brother officers, who attended Dr. Twining's classes; "like myself," he says, "one of the last in the regiment one would ever have thought likely to become religious."

To his brother Edward, too, he writes very affectionately, trying to set before him the religion of Christ in its fairest beauty. He had tried what the pleasures of this world were worth, and found them unsatisfying, even in the heyday of youth and health. "I know," he writes, "I know, like Newton, what the world can do, and what it *cannot* do."

A little after this he begins to keep a diary, and we see how hard he is struggling against evil temper and idleness, and how sorry he feels for having given pain to others by laughing at them, and for indulging in "detestable pride." He makes rules, too, for all the occupations of the day, and for reading and prayer, which, whether they could all be exactly kept or not, show, at all events, that he had fully made up his mind about the service of his Master. Dr. Twining's name is frequently mentioned in the diary, and one day we find a record of Vicars taking the Bible-class, the doctor being ill. This was rather an ordeal, as there were officers present as well as men. In the service of God regimental duties were never neglected; indeed, the young Christian prays, not only for spiritual grace, but for energy in all his daily duties. " Enable me, Lord Jesus," he says, "to please my colonel, and yet to please Thee."

There are those who say that such a prayer is simple mockery, that it is indeed impossible to be at once a soldier of the Cross and a soldier of Queen Victoria. War, they urge, is a cruel, blood-thirsty profession, calling up all manner of evil passions. It is nothing but wholesale murder, and, therefore, horribly wicked. Soldiers are sinners by their very profession, and no Christian can possibly have anything to do with what must be so hateful to a holy God.

A great deal of this, unhappily, is quite true, but surely not all. War may be—alas, often is—horribly wicked, when entered upon from covetousness, pride, or hatred; but at times it is actually *necessary*, and no necessary thing can be wrong, for God never places us in a position where we *must* do wrong. War must be undertaken, sometimes, to maintain the liberty of a country: to defend the right; to rescue the weak and the helpless. Did not England do well, three

hundred years ago, in preparing to resist the arrogant
Spanish invader, and in rejoicing when his ships were
scattered and his army destroyed? Is an insolent
prince to be allowed to trample on the liberties and
the rights of his people, or to defy the laws laid down
for the peace and safety of his realm? Are little innocent children and tender women to be given up tamely
to fire and sword, among brutal idolaters, when the
Mutiny sets India in a blaze, and the path of rescue
must be a path of blood? If these things are to be
suffered rather than the sword be unsheathed, then
every policeman who patiently treads his beat is an
insult to God, and no father has the right to stay the
hand of the murderer stretched out against his own
child!

And if war calls up evil passions, which, alas, it
does, it also brings out all that is noblest and bravest
in the heart of man; for stories of deeds of the most
splendid and unselfish heroism lie thickly scattered
through the pages of all war-chronicles of Christian
nations. If war, then, is needful, of course a Christian
man may be a soldier; he should, indeed, and he *does*
make the *best* soldier. "Havelock's saints" are ready
for the fray at a moment's notice, when many of their
godless companions are drunk or in the guard-house.

Surely, then, no word of condemnation should be
passed on Hedley Vicars because, when he became a
Christian, he did not give up his post in the army.
True, he was called upon to enter on a war which
few would now defend as a righteous or a just one,
but that was the fault of his country; and who will
dare to say that our hapless army, among Crimean
snows, would have fared better, or have fought more

bravely, had all the Christian men in its ranks refused to serve their country because they served their God?

CHAPTER IV.

THE CALL TO ARMS.

IN April 1853 came the welcome news that the 97th Regiment had been ordered home; and having reached England in May, Hedley Vicars writes in June from Walmer Barracks to his dear friend Dr. Twining, from whom he had parted very unwillingly.

Once in old England again, it was tantalizing to be so near home without being able to get leave to go and see his dear ones, from whom he had been parted nearly nine years; but a meeting was impossible for the first few weeks. When at last he reached home, it was quite unexpectedly. All the family were out at week-evening service; and, on their return, great was the surprise and delight with which the long-absent loved one was greeted. Then followed happy weeks with mother and sisters, and little nephews and nieces— weeks, perhaps, all too short for everything there was to hear and to tell after such a long separation, and no doubt, they flitted away much too fast. Most of the time was spent at the house of Vicars' brother-in-law, Lord Rayleigh, though time was found to visit the poor and sick and aged in the village, when the young soldier delighted the hearts of the old women especially by his courteous attention.

In July, Vicars joined his regiment once more on
Chobham Common, near Woking; but in the autumn
he returned again to the family circle. On the
Common the troops lived in tents, not barracks, and
the furniture of the adjutant's tent was certainly not
very rich. A camp-stool, a table with four rough legs,
a camp bedstead, a tub, a portmanteau, and "plenty
of straw, rather mouldy"—these were all the domestic
comforts that Hedley Vicars could boast; but he had
been too long accustomed to the hardships of a soldier's
life to make a trouble of his meagre surroundings.
Besides, it did not last long, for before the end of
August the regiment removed to Canterbury; and
though he was often very lonely and uncomfortable
while at Chobham, there were bright and happy hours
even then. A visit to Spithead to see the naval review was greatly enjoyed; and he speaks with delight
of welcoming a home missionary, Mr. Rigley, to his
tent, and the comfort of talking and praying together.
Vicars found pleasure, too, in showing kindness to
others. One day he noticed two deplorable-looking
fellows picking up what appeared to be bits of rag;
but, on going up to speak to them, he found that
they were so famished that they were eating bits of
meat and biscuit which the soldiers had thrown away
in the mud while at their meals. "I got them," he
says, "some *clean* meat and a loaf, and talked to them
a little." The poor men were quite astonished that a
gaily-dressed officer should take the trouble to care
for them, and to tell them about Christ their Saviour,
and seemed very grateful. One had been dreadfully
maimed while working on the railway, but seemed to
be a Christian, and no doubt always remembered that

pleasant meeting with one who not only professed his Master's name, but cared, like his Master, for the poor and suffering.

The following month mother and son were together again for a little time at Southend, and Mrs. Vicars ventured a good deal on the water with such a strong pair of arms to ply the oars. " There is but little of the *real* thing in the world," writes Vicars shortly after, " and therefore a man values a *mother's* love the more." Fresh friendships were formed during those last months; for in October Vicars first became acquainted with Dr. Marsh of Beckenham, and with his daughter, who was then busily engaged in her work among the navvies, and who, after the death of her young soldier-friend, gave us the only record of his life that has been published. In November, Vicars spent a few days at the rectory, where he taught in the school, read and prayed with the sick, and conducted a little service for the navvies. " I have thought so much of the Bible," said one of the men, " since Captain Vicars told us what it was to him, and how those words about the blood of the Lord Jesus gave him peace." A friend who met him at that visit said, " He speaks as if he had not only spoken to his Saviour, but been answered back again by a living Friend."

In London, Vicars carried on the same loving work for others until his return to Essex, and on the last day of the year he rejoined his regiment in Canterbury. Very soon after he was greatly distressed by his mother's serious illness, but happily . Mrs. Vicars entirely recovered. Death was to spare mother and son a little longer to each other ; and when he parted them, it was to take the young disciple swiftly into the presence of the King.

In February 1854 came a sudden call to leave England, though not on military duty. The uncle of Hedley Vicars, Colonel Edward Vicars, was lying dangerously ill at Gibraltar, and his wife being unable to bear the voyage, his nephew got leave of absence and started off at once. The weather was delightful, and the passage a good one, the *Indus* arriving at Gibraltar in five days; but the ship seems to have been rather crowded, for Vicars could not, as he hoped, have a cabin to himself, and in the company of two young cadets in the East India service, who, very likely, were up to all sorts of pranks, it needed some courage to open a Bible or to kneel down for prayer. The young Christian was, he owned, "strongly inclined to avoid the reproach of the Cross." " It shows," says he, " what a coward I am, that I should, even for an instant, be tempted to hide my colours, and ashamed to confess Christ." But the temptation was overcome and the Master's service boldly avowed : whatever the cadets said or did, there is not a doubt that at the bottom of their hearts they thoroughly admired their comrade's pluck.

On deck Vicars could walk and think undisturbed after his companions had gone to rest, and many a pleasant hour was thus spent during the brilliant moonlight nights on the water. Far happier, too, were his meditations, as he watched the starlit sky and repeated to himself verses of the 19th Psalm, than during that well-remembered voyage across the Atlantic, when the past was a bitter memory, good resolves were made only to be swept away by the

first sneer of a gay companion, and when the Cross
was not yet in sight, nor the heavy burden of sin
rolled away.

But although the vessel came into port in good
time, Hedley Vicars was obliged to wait for seven
days before being allowed to land and hurry to the
side of the sufferer he had come so far to see. There
was so much cholera in Europe that no ship was
suffered to discharge her passengers or cargo till it
was quite certain there were no cases on board which
might bring infection to the shore; so Vicars had to
wait, with what patience he could muster, till the
appointed quarantine was over. When he *did* reach
his uncle's side, he proved an immense comfort and
help to the sick man, whom he nursed and tended
with unwearying care.

While Hedley Vicars had been detained in the port
at Gibraltar, and afterwards waiting on the invalid,
peaceful England had suddenly been aroused to a state
of great excitement. Though she had plenty of
soldiers, and was proud of her smart regiments, it was
very long since she had known anything of actual
warfare, and the news that an army was to be sent
at once to Turkey and the Black Sea came with a
great shock of surprise. Thousands of happy hearts
were suddenly weighed down with a terrible anxiety
and dread, for as regiment after regiment was called
out and embarked for the East, mothers and wives,
sisters and sweethearts, watched, through a mist of
mournful tears, the departure of their loved ones, for
well they knew many would *never* return; *how* many
was happily hidden from their eyes.

Warm as their sympathy might be for others, we

can well imagine that, to the friends of Hedley Vicars, it was always a relief, in scanning the morning paper, to find that the regiments ordered out next for foreign service bore *any* number but that of *ninety-seven*. But the evil day could not long be put off: the figures they so little desired to see in print at length stared them in the face; the 97th was under orders, and Captain Vicars must take up his post of duty, and go forth to the battle-field—to a battle-field, alas, as fatal as any on which the soldier-sons of England have ever fallen. And there was another anxiety. Their friend was already half-way to his destination. Possibly he would join his regiment at Gibraltar, and so they would miss even the sorrowful satisfaction of saying good-bye. But this disappointment was spared them. Early in March, Captain Vicars was again in England.

CHAPTER V.

FAREWELLS.

AND now followed two sorrowful months of preparations and leave-takings.

Hedley Vicars joined his regiment at Windsor on his first return to England. But though under orders, nobody knew exactly where they were going, or why; indeed it was not known till more than a week after sailing, so completely does a soldier often obey commands without being at all aware of their meaning or their object.

At the end of March the captain paid a visit to his

dear friends at Beckenham, and gave an address to a hundred of Miss Marsh's navvies. One of them said afterwards, " He put hisself alongside of us as a fellow-sinner, and yet so good now, and such a *man* too!" It was plain that none of these great sturdy fellows looked on the young captain as "one of your milk-and-water chaps." His earnest words touched them deeply, and at the close of the meeting they crowded round to shake hands and wish safety and success in "foreign parts." "It's a pity such a fine fellow as that should make food for powder," they said among themselves. Several met him alone, out of the way of their comrades, making him a promise he greatly valued—that they would remember to pray for him regularly. Two he met the next morning to talk and pray with, by their own special wish, afterwards going to see a dying navvy at Sydenham. The sick man said of the visit, "I never heard a prayer like that; every word went straight to my heart."

Of his friend Miss Marsh, Hedley Vicars begged one last favour. "When I am shot," said he, as though he had no expectation of ever returning home —"when I am shot, write to my mother; see her when you can, comfort her as God will teach you:" a request which, just one year later, was no doubt sorrowfully but lovingly fulfilled, though at the time it seemed that the young life, for which so much prayer was offered, would surely be spared, even amid scenes of danger and of death.

" Blessed Beckenham," Vicars calls the pretty village where so many happy hours had been spent; and this visit was not to be, as was thought at the time, the last he would pay, for, while quartered at Kensington

Barracks, he came down more than once to see his friends. At a meeting of navvies he then addressed, Captain Vicars told them the story of his conversion, and something of the reckless life he had led, both at Malta and in Jamaica, even when cholera was raging. So watchful was he against sin slyly creeping into his own heart, even at such a time, that, when he had finished speaking, he turned to Miss Marsh and said, "I wish you had not asked me to speak of myself: one is afraid of feeling proud even in telling of one's sins."

It was at this time that Miss Marsh sent him the "Soldier's Prayer," printed on a little card, to give away to any who cared to have it, and which was eagerly welcomed by great numbers, especially in the hospitals during war-time. "Being a soldier," said Vicars, "I take the liberty of using it myself. God grant they may all offer it from their hearts!" The prayer ran thus: "O God, wash me from all my sins in my Saviour's blood, and I shall be whiter than snow. Fill me with the Holy Ghost, for Jesus Christ's sake." Vicars then tells us how, if he had to lead a forlorn hope, he would, if possible, choose Christian men for his battalion; for it was a wicked and dangerous lie to say, "The worse the man the better the soldier."

One very sweet pleasure, in the fulfilment of a hope he had long had in his heart, came to brighten these last sad days; for, only a few weeks before sailing, Hedley Vicars formed a marriage engagement, and the love of the one who then promised to be his wife was a great cheer and comfort to him when far from all he loved, making summer, he tells us, of his dreary winter in the midst of the most appalling wretchedness, suffering, and death.

It was at this time that Hedley Vicars so sturdily denied the necessity for a Christian to cease to be a soldier. He owns that, had he learned to love Christ at seventeen, he would not have chosen such a calling (though it is difficult to imagine how he could have chosen any position where his bright example would better have glorified his Master); but adds these bold and vigorous words: "Do not suppose that, finding a soldier's cross too irksome, I would change it for one less weighty. Never! The Lord God has called me to eternal life in the army, and as a soldier I will die. Death alone shall make me desert my colours."

But even to this steadfast, trusting heart the last partings were a sore trial. To his mother Vicars said farewell on the morning when he came up to London to be ready for immediate orders for embarking, and a few days later he set sail. But during those last few days he found another opportunity for visiting Beckenham, and satisfying the eager desire of the navvies there to hear his voice once more. When the address was over the men seemed as if they could hardly let their friend go, and crowded round for one last grasp of the hand, one tearful "God bless you." One man, unwilling to hinder the captain further by pressing in among the rest, ran after his carriage all the way to the station, hoping for one last glimpse, though in the darkness and confusion his hope was unfortunately disappointed. "If I knew where to find him at Kensington," said the man, "I would go up and see him again."

At last came the actual order for departure. The

regiment was to leave Waterloo Station at six o'clock on the morning of the 19th of May, for embarkation in the *Orinoco.* Some of Vicars' own family, and also friends at Beckenham, had promised they would bid him a last farewell at the station whenever he should leave, and before the *hour* was known the promise had been eagerly claimed. But on the 18th the young captain wrote a loving farewell to his friends, for at such an early hour he could not hope to have the pleasure of seeing them face to face. But real friendship is not easily daunted, and a sweeter sunshine than that of the May morning greeted the traveller as, one by one, dear relations and friends came up to grasp his hand and wish him God-speed as he went forth on his perilous path of duty.

Even in this last hour Vicars could find time to think of the anxieties and farewells of others, as well as of his own. "O Mr. Vicars, you *will* see that Cottrell writes to me reg'lar, won't you?" said a soldier's wife to the young officer, who, she well knew, would not thrust her away as a troublesome intruder. And the poor woman left the station comforted by a few kind words, and no doubt satisfied, too, that her husband had a better chance of "keeping straight" under such a leader than had many of his comrades in other regiments. "Since Mr. Vicars became so good he has steadied nearly four hundred men in the regiment," said a soldier, a short time before, to Miss Marsh. "I don't mean that he has made all the four hundred as good as himself—that he couldn't do: I know enough of religion to know that God alone could do that—but he has sobered and steadied nigh four hundred of the wildest and

most drunken lot. There isn't a better officer in the
Queen's service !"

A few minutes' delay before the starting of the
train gave the little group of friends time to gather
in the waiting-room, and read together a few verses
from the Psalms. Like a tower of strength came these
last words of confidence and hope : "The Lord shall
preserve thy going out and thy coming in from this
time forth, and even for evermore." A few hours
later, and the travellers were on board the *Orinoco;*
though the vessel did not weigh her anchors till a day
or two later, as more troops from Windsor were expected. Vicars despatches a letter at once to his
mother, for it may be long before he has another
chance of writing ; and also one to a kind friend who
had met him at the station. To her he confesses that
he had come on his way with a heavy heart, and had
been thankful to find himself in a carriage alone ;
" for even a soldier may be allowed a few tears at
parting." Cottrell's wife is remembered, a reminder
being given to her husband to write to her.

By the end of the month the *Orinoco* was sailing
up the Mediterranean, and at last it became generally
known for what port the troops were bound. Greece
was to be their destination, and on that shore they
would join some French troops—France and Turkey
being England's allies. This spot was scarcely near
enough to the seat of war to satisfy the ardent spirit
of the young soldier ; but it was many months before
the regiment moved any further eastward ; and the
men, alas, were doomed to endure quite as much severe
hardship and suffering as any fighting in the face of
the foe could have brought them.

When England so gaily sent forth her sons to the war in the heyday of flowers and sunshine, no doubt she thought to welcome them home again, and to crown them with laurels after a grand and glorious victory, long before winter snows should whiten the land or reunited families gather at the Christmas fireside. But, alas, this bright prospect was nothing better than a pleasant dream. Summer bloomed and faded, and winter crept stealthily on, and still our task was scarcely begun; " victory and glory " indeed seemed farther off than ever. Miserable months dragged their weary length along, leaving in their trail dark records of delay, disappointment, woful mismanagement, disaster, and death ; though lit up, it is true, here and there by lurid flashes of wasted heroism, of fruitless successes, and of gallantry that ended in nothing but ghastly slaughter. The year 1855 only lengthened out the sad chronicle ; and when at last the disgraceful and unseemly conflict came to an end, in the summer of 1856, it was only to have this verdict pronounced upon it: " The war has gained for us absolutely nothing that might not have been better secured by wise and friendly negotiation."

But while our hero is sailing up the familiar waters of the Mediterranean, and before we follow him into active service, we must stay a moment and inquire why it is that the 97th Regiment should be summoned to Greece or Turkey at all, and how it has come to pass that a quarrel has sprung up between the British Lion and the Russian Bear.

CHAPTER VI.

THE PESTILENCE THAT WALKETH IN DARKNESS.

WHEN the Crimean War broke out, England had been at peace for forty years—that is to say, she had not been engaged in any European war; and unfortunately, though she little guessed it, she was quite unprepared for the difficult task that she now undertook with such boastful assurance of speedy victory. Not that her soldiers were any less brave or well-disciplined than those who had fought so splendidly on the field of Waterloo, and in that glorious victory broken down for ever the ambitious schemes of the haughty Napoleon. The names of Alma, of Inkermann, and of Balaklava emblazoned on the colours of our regiments prove how brightly shone the valour of the British soldier during the Crimean campaign.

But other things are needed in war besides courage, cash, and skilful commanders. A soldier cannot fight unless he is fed; he cannot keep in health unless he has proper shelter; he cannot recover, when sick or wounded, unless he has medicines, and bandages, and a comfortable bed; he cannot march, or work hard, or fight, unless he has enough rest and sleep; neither can he endure the cold of a Russian winter unless he has warm clothing, strong boots, and plenty of blankets. Now, unfortunately, our soldiers in the Crimea were very ill-supplied with all these necessary things; and therefore, though they had plenty of guns, and swords,

and shot, and shell, the enemy was not beaten, nor
the war ended as soon as it might have been, because
our brave men were frost-bitten, half-famished, worn
out with hard work, and dying by thousands of
cholera, fever, and neglected wounds. Of this sad
scene we shall see more as we follow our hero to the
battle-field; meanwhile let us try to make out why
these great European nations should have fallen to
fighting at all.

Russia and Turkey were never good friends.
Russia, ill-content with all her wide dominions, often
turned a greedy eye toward the beautiful city of
Constantine, Constantinople, lying so near her southern
borders. *Any* excuse would have been good enough
that would have led to the capture of such a prize;
and as a step in that direction, Russia sent troops
across the river Pruth, declared war with Turkey, and
attempted to take possession of the provinces of the
Danube on the western shore of the Black Sea.

But England objected. " No," said Britannia; " Turkey is my friend, my faithful ally, and you shall not
interfere with the Sultan's dominions. If you do, I
shall come and fight you; and my neighbour France
will help me."

This was not exactly what the Emperor Nicholas,
the Czar of Russia, had expected. Prussia and
Austria, much nearer neighbours, were looking on
unconcerned, and letting him do as he liked; and he
had hoped France and England would do the same.
But the Czar would not draw back. Angry disputes
had been going on at the " Holy Places" in Palestine,
between Latin and Greek monks, and he had claimed
authority over all members of the Greek Church.

But Turkey indignantly refused (if indeed a Turk can take his pipe out of his mouth long enough to be indignant about anything). " Palestine," said the Turk, " is mine, and I won't be dictated to." " No, you shan't, you poor, dear, persecuted innocent," echoed England and France with their hands on their swords. " *We'll* see to that. You just tuck up your legs again on your divan, and sip coffee, and smoke your hookah; *we'll* soon settle Russia for you. At the very sight of a few English warships the cowards will all run away."

But " the cowards " didn't. They stood their ground and fought very valiantly, and by the time England had expected to be ringing her bells of victory, she had just discovered that she had rushed, helter-skelter, into a difficult campaign, and had made a fearful mess of it.

Not that, after all, the Turk was such a dear bosom friend of hers that he must be defended at all hazards. His government, everybody knew, was a disgrace to the civilized nations among whom he dwelt. His habits, his tastes, his religion, his laws, his very vices, were all Oriental ; and many people thought that the sooner he was driven back across the Dardanelles or the Bosphorus into Asia, his original home, the better it would be for all respectable folks in his neighbourhood. But still, while he was here, England had reasons of her own for protecting him. She had lent him money, and when people are in our debt we are, naturally, rather anxious they should get on well, so that they may pay us. Then if Russia once got hold of the Danube provinces, she would soon be in Constantinople, and at once have all the commerce of the Black Sea and the eastern end of the

Mediterranean under her thumb. It would never do to allow that, as England carries on an immense trade in that direction, and is by no means disposed to lose it. And there was India to think of. With Russia lording it in the Mediterranean, it was very likely that Britannia might not be able to go to and fro by Suez as she chose; for although the canal was not then made, the route by Suez was an important one, and to have it cut off might mean the loss of our Indian Empire.

These motives, then, were quite strong enough to make England call out her red-coats, and put her hand in her big pocket to pay expenses; so on the 27th of March 1854 war was declared, and troops began to be shipped for the East. The war was very popular; that is to say, everybody thought it a fine thing to be going to fight the Russians. Some attempt was made, to be sure, to prevent hostilities, and to come to a peaceful agreement with Russia; but it all ended in nothing, and the sight of the sturdy, well-drilled regiments marching through the streets excited the enthusiasm of the crowd so much that every one seemed to imagine that battle and victory were almost the same thing, and that British soldiers must, of course, carry everything before them.

We have seen that Hedley Vicars did not embark with his regiment in the *Orinoco* till the 19th of May; but long before then hundreds of soldiers had been despatched through the Mediterranean, Malta was crowded with troops on their way eastward, and the Dardanelles and Bosphorus were alive with steamers and warships; indeed the Allies had sent their fleets into the Black Sea as early as January, and the Cold-

stream Guards left London in February. By the time
Captain Vicars passed the frowning rock of Gibraltar,
no less than 22,000 British soldiers had reached
Turkish shores; some being encamped in the dirty,
tumble-down, dilapidated town of Gallipoli on the
Dardanelles, and the rest at Scutari, on the shores of
Asia Minor, opposite Constantinople, a town afterwards
famous for its military hospital, in which Florence
Nightingale carried on her noble work of tending the
sick and wounded. Before the *Orinoco* touched at
Malta many of these troops had sailed into the Black
Sea and landed at Varna, a seaport on the east coast
of Bulgaria, from whence they were afterwards sent
across to Sebastopol.

The 97th Regiment did not, like many others, dis-
embark at Malta. The vessel reached the harbour on
the 1st of June, but she stayed only a few hours, and
then went straight on to the Piraeus, where the troops
landed. Already some 6,000 French soldiers were
encamped on the hills about six miles from Athens,
and the French flagship thundered out her salutation
as the *Orinoco* entered the harbour.

The weather was now intensely hot, and the young
captain, fresh from an English spring, found military
duties very trying, and any exertion in the middle of
the day almost impossible. The first sight of Athens
was enjoyed by moonlight, when, perhaps, the noble
ruins of the Acropolis look their grandest. After
some little difficulty in finding the way, and waking
up a sleepy sentry, Vicars and his companions succeeded in reaching the ruins. Having thoroughly enjoyed the beautiful scene, they had hoped for a quiet
half-hour " to read a chapter together on the spot

where Paul once preached 'Jesus Christ and him cruci-
fied:'" but the guide would not leave them in peace,
so after a peep at the city lying two hundred feet
below, they reluctantly returned to the camp. Vicars,
however, had so much enjoyed the expedition that he
went again, with another officer, the very next night,
and there read Paul's sermon on Mars' Hill by moonlight. Both on board ship and in tent Vicars con-
trived to gather a few friends for Bible reading; and
no doubt his courage, in boldly confessing the Master
he served, was an immense encouragement and help
to those who were just beginning the Christian race,
and often had to encounter a storm of ridicule from
their companions.

Life in camp during the months of June and July
could not have been very pleasant and interesting, and
no doubt everybody longed for more active service and
for orders to the front. But a foe, alas, was approach-
ing more terrible and far less easily resisted than the
armed Russian. Hot weather, an unhealthy climate,
and unwholesome food had prepared the way for that
most swift and fatal of diseases, Asiatic cholera, and
by the middle of July the French troops were attacked. Very soon the infection spread to the British
army, and one soldier after another sickened and died.
Twenty-seven fell victims in a week, and before five
weeks had passed *a hundred and twenty* of the finest
men in the regiment were dead.

There was no minister to comfort the sick and the
dying, or to bury the dead; so, as far as his strength
held out, the young Christian captain fulfilled both
these duties, often undertaking funerals for other
officers, a task they gladly escaped. In the poisonous

air of the crowded hospital, or by the grave-side, nearly the whole of the month was spent; and yet, though in deadly peril day by day, the brave Vicars escaped the terrible infection. Not that he was by any means regardless of danger, although he tried to soothe the alarm of his friends. If death must come, he hoped for "a soldier's death, for death in this form," he owned, "has gloom, even for the Christian; but then the sting," he added, "is *for them* completely taken away."

The French, meanwhile, were suffering dreadfully. They lost 700 men and five officers; while the troops at Varna, in Bulgaria, fared no better. Hundreds of Greeks, Turks, French, and English were dying there of this dreadful scourge, while many more were so weakened by illness as to be quite unfit for duty. An expedition sent out by the French from Varna against the Russians met with a most terrible fate. Not only was it a failure on the field of battle, but cholera attacked the troops quite suddenly, and in *eight hours* nearly 600 men died. Before the return to Varna the French had lost no less than 7,000 men.

At the end of August cholera gradually abated in the Piraeus, and by September it had happily quite disappeared. Hedley Vicars now felt that he might have a little holiday, and greatly enjoyed a trip across to Pentelicus, a town on the *east* coast of Attica, looking toward the islands of the Archipelago and the coast of Asia Minor. Here tents were pitched for a few days, among beautiful trees and mountain torrents; and while the young captain rejoices in having exchanged scenes of pestilence and death for such lovely surroundings, he notices also, with thanksgiving, that one of the younger officers, with whom he had often played many a foolish prank, is now listening to the call of Christ and joyfully rising up to follow him.

Before the end of the month, however, Vicars is back once more in his old quarters in the Piræus, in the midst of gloom and rain and tempest; often, too, in complete solitude, for he speaks in one of his letters of "a little quail" as his only companion. His health was not then very good, for though he had escaped any attack of fever or cholera, his constant attendance in the hospitals, and his devoted care for his men, had tried his strength a good deal; and when he felt weak and ill, and especially when he heard of the illness of dear ones in England, he would sometimes grow sad and lose a little of his bright faith. Another trouble, too, puzzled and distressed him much. Letters from home, till now so frequent and regular, suddenly ceased. It seems that his regiment had been ordered to leave for the Crimea, and this order being known in London early in October, Hedley Vicars' friends, thinking he had sailed, posted their letters to the camp before Sebastopol, and were sadly grieved to find, when the next mail came in, that Vicars was still in Greece, and most anxiously looking for news. By that time, however, the camp in the Piræus was all astir, and the young captain's thoughts turned away for a time from his own troubles in the midst of the bustle of departure, and the excitement of a long-expected call to the front. Strength and courage and faith had all returned, and even happiness and peace; for although distressed sometimes at the thought of the grief his death might bring to those he loved, he is perfectly calm and confident for himself, having *no* fear of any fate that might be in store. He is delighted, too, with the decided improvement in the conduct of his men. He had often reproved them for swearing, but could now pass through a whole "tour of duty" and not hear one oath. Whether Christians or not, the men felt they could not take God's name in vain in the face of his bold and faithful servant.

On the 15th of November the 97th embarked, and gladly leaving the shores of Greece behind them, sailed through the Sea of Marmora, encountered some stormy weather in crossing the Black Sea, and then, landing on the south coast of the Crimea on the 19th, went up to join the army under Lord Raglan before Sebastopol.

CHAPTER VII.

FACING THE FOE.

IF it can be said that any "glory" was attached to that most disastrous campaign of 1854–6, all the most glorious battles of the Crimean War had been fought and won before Captain Hedley Vicars set foot on Russian soil.

While the young officer was patiently awaiting his call to the front, comforting and tending the sick and dying, and burying the dead, on Grecian shores, the allied armies of France and England had been meeting their foe in deadly strife. Early in September, the troops had left the plague-stricken camp at Varna and its neighbourhood, and sailed eastward in a magnificent armada of battle-ships and transports, our army numbering 27,000 men, and that of the

French about 24,000. After a good deal of delay and discomfort in landing, thousands of men being exposed all night on the beach to drenching rain, the regiments marched, in splendid battle array, against the enemy, and a skirmish took place immediately. This was followed, a day or two after, by a victorious engagement with the Russians, on the banks of the river Alma, in which many hundreds of brave men were killed, and acres of ground covered with wounded—English, French, Turks, and Russians ; but "'twas a famous victory." The "famous victory," however, did not appear to result in anything particular ; at all events, it was not speedily followed, as every one hoped it would be, by the capture of Sebastopol and the close of the war ; nor, indeed, did it enable our victorious army to secure supplies for themselves and their horses, though there was abundance to be had in the neighbourhood.

About the 26th of September the army reached Balaklava, a dirty little fishing-village to the south-east of Sebastopol. English ships lay in its small harbour ; English sailors had taken possession of its lighthouse ; no resistance was, therefore, offered to the entrance of Lord Raglan's troops. The siege of Sebastopol now began, and on the 25th of October was fought the battle of Balaklava, with its famous charge of the Light Brigade, when, in obedience to some mistaken orders, six hundred horsemen charged the enemy's guns through the "valley of death," and were nearly cut to pieces.

The battle of Inkermann followed on the 5th of November, occasioned by a desperate assault of the Russians on the allied armies, and only resisted by

(3) · 4

very hard fighting and great bloodshed. Although, by this time, "the fall of Sebastopol" had been confidently reported in England, all hopes were now given up of taking the city and getting back into comfortable quarters in the Bosphorus before Christmas. Preparations were, therefore, being made to pass the winter in camp; and Hedley Vicars arrived just in time to share the terrible hardships and sufferings endured by the miserable troops during those dreadful months.

When the *Orinoco* steamed into the harbour of Balaklava with the 97th Regiment on board, the waters of the little bay, though quite placid and peaceful, were strewed in all directions with fragments of wreck, and the beach covered with the remains of the cargoes of the unfortunate vessels that had just been utterly destroyed. On the 14th, the most furious gale ever known to many old sailors accustomed to the savage fury of the blasts on the Black Sea had swept down on the south of the Crimea. That part of the camp of the allied armies pitched in exposed situations was entirely destroyed, nearly every tent being blown down, and a great many swept clean away into the sea. Officers and men—sick and well—all shared together the terrors and the sufferings of that dreadful night, huddling together in a few wretched huts or crowded stables, drenched, mud-covered, famished, and benumbed with cold; some, indeed, dying before morning broke. Mr. W. H. Russell says, in describing the scene: "Imagine the bleakest common in all England, the wettest bog in all Ireland, the dreariest moor in all Scotland, overhung by leaden skies, and lashed by a tornado of sleet, snow, and rain—a few broken stone walls and roofless huts dotting it here and there, roads turned into torrents of mud and water; and then think of the condition of men and horses in such a spot on a November morning, suddenly deprived of their frail covering, and exposed to the bitter cold with empty stomachs, and without the remotest prospect of obtaining food or shelter."

At sea, matters were, if possible, even worse. No less than twenty-one ships were either sunk or seriously damaged, and immense quantities of stores, badly needed by the men, utterly destroyed. Ten million rounds of ammunition went down in one ship alone, and enough hay was spoiled to have fed the starving horses for three weeks. The victorious invaders had so entirely suffered themselves to be shut in by the foe whom they had beaten, that, with miles of haystacks in sight, they were compelled to get all their fodder from England. Pressed hay, worth £5 a ton here, cost the British nation £20 before the poor famishing beasts got a welcome bite. While England knew her victorious army to be surrounded by pastures and farms, and received the news of "glorious victories," she was naturally surprised to be expected to send out to her troops every scrap of food they required, and even fuel; indeed it was absolutely impossible to supply it quickly enough. We had hospitals and magazines of stores at Scutari; but to convey the food *from* the one, and the sick *to* the other, was often a matter of great difficulty. Even when stores came safely into the harbour of Balaklava, they very often did not reach the troops encamped on the heights for weeks afterwards, or

were even *sent back* to the Bosphorus, because there
were no hands for unlading, or no official who could
give orders regarding a particular cargo, or else the
one who was there made some ridiculous blunder.
In this way medicines and hospital stores were
actually carried away again from the sick and
wounded. Stretchers could not be obtained, because
the canvas was in one ship and the frames in another.
Cabbages floated about in the sea and lime-juice
waited in the ships, while the men were dying of
scurvy for the want of them both. Tents that were
needed in November arrived in April, and immense
stores of warm clothing lay idle while the men were
shivering in rags.

The Russians, meanwhile, were much better off;
for, while more accustomed to a cold climate, they
were well sheltered within the walls of Sebastopol.
The French, too, who had a good harbour close to
their camp, were well supplied with all they needed,
thanks to the better management of their War
Department at home; besides, a French soldier is *far*
cleverer at cooking and making the best of his
rations than is an English one.

The British army, then, was in miserable plight
when Hedley Vicars landed on the 20th of November, a pouring wet evening, and marched, or rather
waded through the mud with his regiment to the
encampment, "the men," he tells us, "looking more
like drowned rats than live soldiers." Blazing camp-
fires, for which the wrecked vessels had furnished
abundant fuel, were the only cheerful feature in the
dismal scene; but the captain speaks hopefully to his
men, and the men respond with hearty cheers, in

spite of all their discomfort. The flickering light of
his first bivouac fire flashed on the pages of Vicars'
open Bible that night, as, with a friend, he read the
23rd, 90th, and 91st Psalms; and then, with a bed
of dry leaves (an unusual luxury, for seldom was
anything dry), and a stone for a pillow, he "went to
sleep securely," and "but for the biting cold," would
have "slept like a top."

Two days later, the 97th joined the allied armies
before Sebastopol, after "a rough march of seven
miles," the road being strewn with shot and shell
and dead horses. Alas, it was that "rough march of
seven miles" that often cut off the unfortunate British
army from sorely-needed supplies, even when provisions had reached Balaklava, and had actually been
landed. The road was nothing but a miserable Tartar
cattle-track, passable enough in summer, but lapsing
into a vast puddle of sticky clay directly the winter
rains fell, and along which it became almost impossible
to drag wheels of any description. There had been
some talk of making a proper road, and an abundance
of small stones at hand would have supplied suitable
material; but labour was very scarce, soldiers could
not be spared from fighting to turn navvies, and
though Turkish workmen might be hired, they died
so fast that the one half was pretty well occupied in
burying the other half. Besides, it was never sup-
posed that anything so mad as an attempt to winter
British troops on the open downs of Crim Tartary
would ever be permitted. *Of course*, by the time
winter came, they would all be safe in Sebastopol.

But they were *not*. Opportunities, if such there
had been, were allowed to slip by. Sebastopol, in-

stead of being at once attacked and taken while our
armies were flushed with victory, was suffered to
strengthen her defences and to defy her foes; and
British troops, while spending a dismal enough Christmas in the trenches and the tents, awaited the
onslaught of those two terrible generals on whom the
Czar relied to vanquish his enemies—General January
and General February.

<hr>

CHAPTER VIII.

IN THE TRENCHES.

" WE are all anxiously waiting for Lord Raglan
to storm Sebastopol." So writes Hedley
Vicars at the close of November 1854; and it was not
till *March* that any determined attempt was made to
take the city, and not till the following September
that it was actually captured.

But it was natural enough for any soldier to long
for, and to expect, immediate action, to end the weary
suspense of watching and waiting and serving in the
trenches, in the midst of all sorts of hardships, and
with splendid troops being thinned daily by the
ravages of fever and cholera, which had once more
broken out among them. Sebastopol was the chief
naval arsenal of Russia, and therefore a very strong
and important position. In its harbour all the fleets
of Europe might float securely; but its fortifications,
very formidable ones in 1855, were destroyed when
the town was taken.

Duty in the trenches was now becoming very hard, and as the weather grew colder it became yet more fatiguing, especially as the men often had no rest for several nights in succession. A military "trench" is a shallow ditch with a bank of earth thrown up, and is used to protect soldiers when they wish to get near to a town they are besieging, and would be exposed without its shelter to the enemy's fire.

Food, of a sort, was plentiful enough as yet, and if one was content with such dainties as salt pork and biscuits, biscuits and salt pork, one need not starve; but water was very scarce, and often not to be had at all for washing. For a day or two Vicars "had not water enough to fill a bath for a midge," and was delighted when he secured a pint wherewith to wash a very dirty face and hands.

But, in spite of every discomfort, the little gatherings for Bible-reading and prayer still kept up, proving a help and solace in the midst of troubles; and when a quiet night's rest is occasionally enjoyed, Vicars tells us how pleasantly he dreams of home, even though he may wake up to find his teeth chattering with cold, a sharp stone sticking into his side, and the howling of the wind without mingling with the roar of shot and shell.

Long letters, in spite of all difficulties, were despatched to England on landing in the Crimea, and were written, too, in good spirits; for Vicars was thankful to get away from Greece, and a great packet of home letters which he found awaiting him proved a most welcome treasure. But the inaction before Sebastopol soon proved quite as trying as being "shelved in the Piræus." "We must go at it, hammer and tongs," said he. "The men are dispirited, naturally enough, by losing so many of their comrades from cholera. I can answer for it, they would soon cheer up if they were led against the Russians." And not only were the men out of heart, but also their officers—a good many, indeed, resigning their commissions, against whom Vicars cries shame; though probably they were not such dastards after all if they disapproved, as they well might have done, both of the war itself, and of the way in which it was conducted.

The idea of a "happy Sabbath" being possible under such conditions seems strange indeed, yet Vicars speaks of spending one; for he possessed all the secret of peace and joy within his own heart, and was not dependent on beautiful churches, or noble music, or worshipping throngs for communion with the Master he loved. Indeed, he speaks of never having found his Saviour nearer than in the loneliness of the trenches or the tent, and "when, I should like to know," he adds, "could one find a Saviour more precious than when bullets are falling around like hail?"

What those trenches were it is almost impossible for us to imagine. Very often they were "two or three feet deep in mud, snow, and half-frozen slush; and here, while bullets whizzed around them, the men were on duty fifteen hours together, without nearly enough clothing, and often with boots nearly dropping off their feet. The stoves were wretched affairs that would not burn charcoal at all; or, if they did, were dangerous to warm a tent, as the fumes would be pretty sure to suffocate the sleepers. Several officers indeed *did* lose their lives in this way. It was frequently impossible to get any other fuel, or, if brushwood could be cut for cooking, it must be done at the risk of life, under the fire of the enemy; for the bill-hooks, with which it could have been quickly collected, lay packed in a ship down in the harbour, awaiting the order for unlading.

But amid all these privations, Hedley Vicars had very little complaint to make about his own sufferings, and was anxious to secure, as far as possible, the comfort of his men, patiently sleeping himself on his bed of stones and leaves, giving up his tent to those who, he thought, needed it more, and spending many hours in the miserable hospital tents, now thronged with cholera cases as well as with wounded patients, for in seven weeks no less than 8,000 sick and wounded were sent down to Balaklava, and thence to Scutari. Few ever returned; numbers never survived the horrors of the journey.

And not only were all these hardships endured with unwavering courage and patience, but they were brightened with cheerful good-humour, every little comfort being received with joyous thanksgiving. Some onions, potatoes, a ham, bread, and rancid salt butter, were hailed with delight and made quite a feast, while " soaked biscuit fried in lard " is described as a capital dish. The arrival, too, of a fur rug from England is acknowledged with the warmest gratitude, the welcome gift forming a most valuable addition to the bed of leaves and stones. Hedley Vicars seems also to have found out a fact that very few people were then prepared to believe—namely, that drinking spirits " makes a man colder than ever an hour afterwards." In mistaken kindness, an abundance of rum

was supplied to our unfortunate soldiers, and, of
course, eagerly consumed; but there is no doubt it
was the means of sending hundreds into the hospital
who, without it, would have withstood the cold much
more successfully. "I never drink the half of mine,"
says Vicars; "often none at all." This abstinence
probably accounted, in some measure, for his more
healthy condition, and his safety in the midst of
cholera infection.

All through December the British troops vainly
longed day by day for orders to storm the fortress.
"There is great talk now about our soon going ahead
to storm," writes Vicars. "I trust they will not
delay much longer." But except sorties on the part
of the Russians, and furious cannonading on either
side, nothing was done, and the "hope deferred" made
many a brave heart sick. The weary time of waiting
was well employed by Vicars in reading and talking
to his men of the Christ he served, and he was delighted to find great numbers of them eager to hear
what he had to say. He was looking forward also
to the arrival of good Duncan Matheson, the soldiers'
missionary; for scarcely any chaplains were now left,
and if they had all been at their posts in perfect
health they could not have reached half the men. "I
am so longing," Vicars says, "that every soldier before
he dies should be told of Jesus and all he has done
for him."

Christmas day must have passed gloomily enough
in camp, for many of the stores sent out by England
to her soldier sons did not reach them for months
afterwards; and if they had, there was little opportunity to cook Christmas fare, or even to eat it in

any comfort. But one bright ray of sunshine fell to Hedley Vicars' lot on the joyous festival, that most precious treasure, a home-letter, being handed in; and he writes at once a few lines in reply, although the intense cold made it difficult to hold a pen. The letter came very near to being the last one he ever wrote, for early in January Captain Vicars nearly lost his life while quietly sleeping in his tent.

After a fearful night in the snowy trenches he had ventured to indulge in a small charcoal fire, telling his servant to leave the tent door partly open to admit fresh air. But the deadly fumes overpowered him as he lay, and when his servant called him to prepare for afternoon duty he could not be aroused, and help was quickly summoned. The doctor had just visited another tent where an officer lay dead from the very same cause; and when Vicars, quite insensible, was carried out and laid on the snow, his men gathered round in the greatest despair and grief, fully believing he was dead. But after a great deal of rubbing, and *in spite of* the violent remedies of blistering and bleeding then in fashion, signs of life once more appeared; and though laid aside for several weeks by serious illness, the patient finally recovered, having been most tenderly and lovingly nursed by Lieutenant Douglas Macgregor.

By the 12th of January Vicars was once more at his wearisome work in the trenches, though still far from strong; but the regiment was now so thinned by disease that the work fell very heavily on those still able to serve at all. Nothing more had been done toward taking the fortress, and there certainly seemed no prospect whatever of reducing the place simply by the fire of artillery; meanwhile frost and snow continued to work deadly havoc among the men. February opened with no brighter outlook regarding military matters, though the weather, if still cold, was fine, which cheered the spirits of the men, and more warm clothing arrived, which, even at this late hour, was extremely welcome. But Vicars' brave spirit refused to be depressed by any gloomy forebodings. "Although," he writes, "I have seen many a noble soldier laid low for ever, and regiments reduced to less than half their number by sickness, since the 20th of November, I have no fear of the eventual result, by the help of God." But he sees now that the taking of Sebastopol will be "an affair of several months;" though he has the audacity to expect some "rather good fun" in the trenches when only the warm weather comes. He acknowledges, too, kind presents received for the men, one lady having cut up her fur cloak into chest-preservers for them, another supplying a number of needle-books and scissors. A Christian navvy from Beckenham, then a private soldier in a distant part of the camp, rejoiced the heart of Hedley Vicars by his service among the sick, and was gladly welcomed in his tent, which the owner describes as quite a mansion, possessing a *fire-place* which smokes only two or three times a day, a chair, a table made out of a cask, and, best of all, that fur on the bed, which is "the envy of all who see it."

Two more boxes of comforts for the men arrived in February, and gave immense satisfaction, not only to the happy possessors of warm garments, but to the young captain who had the delightful duty of distributing them. A parcel of books from home was

brought up from Balaklava by Duncan Matheson,
whose visit was like a gleam of heavenly sunshine.
The two talked and prayed for nearly an hour. " I
feel still," said Vicars, writing afterwards, " the blessing
of that visit." He rejoiced, too, that three brother
officers standing by must have heard the prayer of
that devoted servant of God. The books, and Testa-
ments, and prayer-cards sent from England were
gladly welcomed by the soldiers; for they had very
few among their officers to speak to them of the life
to come, and Captain Vicars, not content with minis-
tering only to his own regiment, made a " tour " round
all the hospitals to carry cards of prayer for each
patient. Two other treasures also arrived from home.
One was a candle-stove, doubtless considered a very
clever and perfect arrangement before we had learned
to cook so well with oil, and Vicars was delighted
with the help it afforded in preparing meals, and
offered the use of it to his friends. The other gift,
hardly less valued, was a sketch of Beckenham church
and rectory, recalling the happy days passed with Dr.
Marsh and his family, and awakening fresh hopes of
soon seeing home and beloved ones once more. Alas,
they were never to be fulfilled on earth !

CHAPTER IX.

BEULAH-LAND

MARCH opened cold and frosty. Even now the
vast supplies of warm clothing despatched
from England had not reached all the troops, and

men were still to be seen wading about in the mud and ice without *any soles* to their boots; many, in consequence, being disabled by frost-bites. But, in the intervals of frost and snow, spring peeped out. The 5th of March, Vicars tells us, was "a lovely summer's day. But then," he adds, "to-morrow it may be snowing." Wild-fowl appeared in the harbour; flocks of pretty song-birds well known in England—goldfinches, larks, and linnets—fluttered about the camp, twittering merrily in the bushes between the roar of the cannon; while pale snowdrops forced up their delicate white bells and tiny spikes of green between the crannies of huge piles of shot, or gay crocuses peered out from under deadly shells. The few fruit-trees that were left put out their cheerful blossoms, budding foliage appeared on the hillsides, and the muddy, trampled plain began to take a faint tinge of green here and there.

By the middle of the month things were looking decidedly brighter. The men were healthier and more hopeful. Seven hundred huts had been put up; a telegraph was in working order; a railway had been laid down; bakeries were at work supplying wholesome food; fresh meat and vegetables were coming in freely; and comforts arrived in such quantities from England that the camp was "a sea of abundance" of all necessaries, from huts and sheepskins down to respirators and jujubes! No progress, however, seemed to have been made with the siege; for if the English troops had now struggled through the worst of their troubles, the Russians had all the while been greatly strengthening their position, and the united fire of the Allies availed nothing to force them to sur-

render. The Emperor Nicholas was dead. This
event did not, however, appear to damp the ardour
of our foe, who went on throwing up batteries and
sending out sorties not quite so unsuccessfully as the
besiegers could have wished.

This kind of thing went on for months; but as our
hero had no share in the final struggle and the closing
victory, we shall not attempt further to follow the
history of this terrible war. To make our story complete, however, it may just be added that, after the
failure of several bombardments and assaults, the great
fortress was at last taken on the 8th of September
1855, the French attacking the Malakoff and the
British the Redan, the two great forts of the city.
The Malakoff was captured; and though the British
attack was repulsed at the time, the Russians retreated,
blowing up their magazines, and setting fire to the city,
leaving its ruins in the hands of the Allies. Lord
Raglan had died some three months before, General
Simpson taking the command of the army. After the
capture of Sebastopol, this commander received the
Grand Cross of the Legion of Honour. But the war
was not even then over, the allied armies remaining
on Russian soil for another ten months. Some sea-
fighting took place, and General Simpson was succeeded
by General Codrington. An armistice was concluded in
February 1856, followed in April by the proclamation
of peace. In July the last British regiment sailed out
of the Black Sea, and Europe was at peace.

But to return. In February and March 1855 we
find Hedley Vicars busy visiting his men in hospital,
and taking "John Carthy" jam and biscuit. Jam and
marmalade had always been greatly in demand, because

they were so easily carried. Butter, when provisions were scarce, if it was to be had at all, was packed in immense crocks that needed a waggon to move them; and W. H. Russell tells us how "Captain Smith, a famished wretch," might have been seen, dressed in any odds and ends on which he could lay his hands, the whole "topped by a head-dress *à la dustman of London*, stalking gravely through the mud of Balaklava, intent on the capture of a pot of jam or marmalade." Of course any little comforts of this kind were doubly acceptable to the sick in hospital.

Sundays do not pass without little services in camp and hospital, and the writing of long and loving letters to home friends, with bright accounts of the writer's health and happiness. "Sickness," he says, "is on the decrease, and we are all as lively as kittens." Truly it is the heart at peace with God, and loyal to his service, that can afford to be always cheerful. But although there were fewer victims of disease, men continued to fall by shot and shell while defending the trenches. In his very last letter home Hedley Vicars deplores the sudden death of one of them, a Christian captain belonging to the Engineers. He tells also how his company had been turned out in readiness for action, as the French were making an attack on a Russian advanced work. After half-an-hour's "standing to arms," all was quiet, and the company returned to their tents, *nothing* whatever having been accomplished, except the slaughter of two hundred French soldiers, and probably of at least as many Russians.

Vicars is very glad to hear of a day being appointed in England for national prayer, and promises that it shall also be kept in the tents. Had England prayed as earnestly for *peace* as she did for *victory,* her prayers, doubtless, would have been more speedily answered. Captain Vicars' last Sabbath on earth was passed, as usual, in hospital-visiting, reading, and prayer; and on the day of national prayer, the 21st of March, he conducted the services himself. A friend who passed the evening with him tells us that the young soldier seemed, like Christian in the " Pilgrim's Progress," to have reached his Beulah-land, which indeed he had, walking in that country where " the sun shineth night and day," which is " beyond the Valley of the Shadow of Death," and also out of the reach of Giant Despair; " there, " drawing near to the city, he had yet a more perfect view thereof." At night he writes: " I have felt this day to be just like Sunday, and have derived much comfort from communion with my God and Saviour." Then he speaks of his friend Cay, and tells how he had walked with him, and " exchanged thoughts about Jesus." At this word he pauses, laying down his pen after writing the name so dear in life and in death. He never took up that pen again. He had just written, " In Jesus I find all I want of happiness or enjoyment, and as weeks and months roll by, I believe he is becoming more and more lovely in my eyes."

That altogether lovely One stood close at hand. The thin veil that parted the all-glorious Master from his loyal, loving disciple was just about to be rent asunder. The traveller, whose " moving tent " had been so often pitched " a day's march nearer home," had now indeed, though he knew it not, but one day's march left between him and the eternal city. A few hours more, and, " absent from the body," he would be "at home with the Lord." Could those who loved him best refuse, even in the midst of their tears, the submissive, nay, the joyful response?—

> " For ever with the Lord !
> Amen—so let it be !
> Life from the dead is in that word ;
> 'Tis immortality."

CHAPTER X.

VICTORY.

ALTHOUGH the British army was now in a very much better condition than it had been during the dreadful winter of exposure and hardship, the great losses it had suffered threw very heavy work upon those men who were still fit for duty. Very often the trenches were so imperfectly defended that, had the Russians known exactly the weak points, a sudden attack would have met with hardly any resistance.

The French position, meanwhile, had been greatly strengthened by the arrival of fresh troops ; but our numbers fell sadly short, and the men were obliged to be on duty in the trenches for twenty-four hours at a stretch, and were only allowed three nights out of seven for sleep. Where 1,200 or 1,500 soldiers were needed, it was only possible to place 900, and therefore the men were so far apart that, at a spot watched eagerly by our foes for a chance of driving us out, it would have been scarcely possible to resist an unexpected rush of the enemy.

On the night of the 22nd a desperate fight suddenly broke out. As one of the officers of the Royal Artillery wrote, "It was Inkermann on a small scale —an attack in very great force and at all points." Everything had been very still just before, but 8,000 Russians had crept near the French works in the evening, sheltering themselves in little hollows, and waiting for the darkness of night to cover their further advance. Between eleven and twelve o'clock they dashed in upon the French so suddenly and in such strength that, in spite of a stout resistance, they succeeded in driving back our allies, marching on immediately toward the British trenches without being at first recognized.

Hedley Vicars discovered, however, that the moving columns were Russians not French, and prepared at once to receive their desperate onslaught. Lying down in obedience to orders, the men suffered the enemy to approach quite close; and then, leaping to their feet, and led by their noble young captain, the gallant little band of but two hundred men, after pouring in a volley of shot, charged right ahead in the teeth of an attacking force of two thousand. Though wounded by a Russian bayonet, Captain Vicars sprang on the parapet of the trenches, and shouting, "Men of the 97th, follow me!" dashed down the slope in the face of the foe, followed closely by his men, and waving his flashing sword in the fitful moonlight. Once more his clear, strong, ringing war-cry rent the air, as he rushed forward. "This way, 97th!" cried the young captain; and "this way" came on the 97th right bravely, driving back, at the point of the bayonet, the surging throng of foes. On to victory they came; for after an hour's hard fighting the enemy was beaten, and the hill-side covered with their dead. But the victory had been dearly won, for the allies lost sixteen officers and more than two hundred men.

To the unutterable grief of the men of the 97th, their beloved young captain, Hedley Vicars, fell in the dreadful rush while almost his first battle-cry had scarcely died on his lips, his dauntless courage defying all the terrors of wounds and death. He fell, too, among his foes; but friends quickly fought their way to his side, and saved him at once from being either taken prisoner or lying uncared for on the blood-stained field. Tenderly lifting their wounded comrade, they carried him back towards his tent, meeting Captain Browne on the way, who placed his friend on a stretcher and brought him water, the last service Hedley Vicars ever received from human hands.

Alas, no one knew the nature of his injury, nor the kind of aid to render, or possibly, even in that extremity, the young life might have been spared. He had been struck in the right arm, close to the shoulder, the ball cutting in two a main artery, from which the life-blood ebbed only too fast, unchecked, and probably unseen, in the midnight darkness. Even the wounded man himself was, at first, quite unaware of danger. He assured his anxious friends that his hurt was but slight, and that he should soon recover, until, as they carried him forward, though apparently not suffering much pain, he was warned by increasing exhaustion that his life was failing fast. Chilled by the loss of blood and by exposure to the night air, he asked for his cloak.

But that chill was the chill of death. "Cover my face," he said, a few minutes after, "cover my face." It has been thought by some that these words were spoken by the dying Christian as he suddenly felt himself nearing the presence of a holy God, the darkness of night being, surely, a sufficient screen from the eyes of his fellow-men. It may have been so; but it seems more probable that, with a tender regard for the feelings of others, and, perhaps, forgetful of the darkness on which his eyes had for ever closed, he was anxious that those who loved him should not see the shadow of death gather on his face. Although always ready to own his utter unworthiness in God's sight, Hedley Vicars had absolutely *no* fear of death, or of standing in the presence of the God he loved and served; and his heart, instead of trembling, must have been thrilled with joy at the thought of meeting his Saviour face to face, and knowing even as he was known.

Just before the soldiers set down their sad burden at the tent-door, the sweet light of the everlasting day-dawn broke, at the moment of earth's dreariest midnight. Leaving the bright imprint of a happy smile on the tranquil face, the redeemed spirit passed upward to its God, amid choirs of welcoming angels; and when Lieutenant Macgregor entered the tent a few minutes after, distressed at the sad news that his beloved friend was wounded, he looked upon the face of the dead.

Brave soldier that he was, Douglas Macgregor wrote to his mother thus, the next day, "My heart is wrung, my eyes are red and hot with crying. I feel gloomy and sorrowful altogether. My very dear friend Vicars was killed last night!" And then he goes on to tell how tenderly he loved his friend, how brightly that friend had lived as a Christian, and how nobly he had died. "I know not how to live without him," he says; "he was my truest friend, my most cheerful companion." Blinded with tears, and well-nigh broken-hearted at his loss, Douglas Macgregor cut a lock of the curling brown hair, and loosened from the neck of the dead soldier a tiny gold locket. This locket contained the portrait of one whom Hedley Vicars fondly loved, and ever since it had reached him, just as he left Greece in November, it had been worn next his heart. Now, stained with his life-blood, it was sent back, according to his wish, to his sorrowing friends in England, together with a little book of Psalms, his constant companion.

Not for very long were these loving friends to be parted. Six months after, on that terrible day when, at the cost of hundreds of lives, Sebastopol was taken, Lieutenant Macgregor took part in a desperate but unsuccessful attempt to storm the Redan. Having twice fought his way into the fortress, he fell there among the dreadful heaps of slain, together with four other officers of the 97th Regiment, thus, by the red path of battle, entering, like his beloved companion, on the land of everlasting peace.

Great was the grief of the private soldiers of the 97th at the loss of a leader they all honoured and loved. Several of them, in their letters home, speak of Captain Vicars with the warmest admiration and devotion. Close to the mile-stone on the Woronzoff road to Sebastopol a few of them dug his grave, and, on the afternoon of the 24th, tenderly laid him to rest in that lovely spot, all the officers of the 97th, and a great number of men, besides friends from other regiments, being present at the solemn funeral service. Dr. Cay afterwards had a stone set up to mark the grave, bearing these words—"In memory of Captain Vicars, 97th Regiment, who was killed in the sortie from Sebastopol, 22nd March 1855. Erected by his sorrowing comrades."

The little mound, among the many rows marking like resting-places, was carefully tended by rough but kindly hands. The men bordered it with stones and shells, and planted sweet flowers in the stiff clay, the warm spring sunshine soon swelling the green buds and brightening the sad spot with cheerful blossoms, fit emblems of the glorious resurrection of the dead, when that which is sown in weakness shall be raised in power.

The last words spoken to his men by Captain Hedley Vicars are memorable ones when we think of what his character was, and how anxiously he tried to lead others in the same narrow path he was treading, and to guide their feet into the way of peace. "This way, 97th!" may well ring in our ears; for the young Christian's path was ever straight forward in "the way that leadeth unto life," turning neither to the right hand nor to the left, even in the midst of fierce temptation; and that path of the just which, on earth, was as a shining light, has brightened now into the perfect day in the street of that city where "they need no candle, neither light of the sun; for the Lord God giveth them light: and they shall reign for ever and ever."

Looking one day to meet that faithful young soldier of Christ in the bright home where, with so many others who have fought a good fight and kept the faith, he waits to welcome us, let us send up from our hearts the prayer of Duncan Matheson, the soldiers' missionary and Hedley Vicars' friend— "Lord, more grace, more grace, that we may follow him as he followed Jesus."

THE END.